201 WAYS TO

SAY NO GRACEFULLY AND EFFECTIVELY

ALAN AXELROD AND JIM HOLTJE

McGraw-Hill

New York   San Francisco   Washington D.C.   Auckland   Bogotá   Caracas   Lisbon   Madrid
Mexico City   Milan   Montreal   New Delhi   San Juan   Singapore   Sydney   Tokyo   Toronto

McGraw-Hill

*A Division of The **McGraw·Hill** Companies*

1 2 3 4 5 6 7 8 9 0   DOC/DOC   9 0 2 1 0 9 8 7

ISBN 0-07-006219-6

10.95 PB

This book is printed on recycled, acid-free paper containing a
minimum of 50% recycled, de-inked fiber.

Other Quick-Tip Survival Guides:

201 Ways to Manage Your Time Better

201 Ways to Deal With Difficult People

CONTENTS

QUICK START

The folks flipping burgers at the fast-food joint are the last of the 9-to-5ers. The forty-hour week? In your dreams. Try *sixty hours*. Minimum.

Hours. There aren't enough of them. Succeeding in business has always been a tough go. These days, it's downright brutal. What do you need most?

All the help you can get.

What do you need even more?

Time.

The Quick-Tip Survival Guides put the two together, giving you all the help you need—without taking all the time you have.

Here is a series for today's business reader. A reader pressed by a hundred demands and pulled in a dozen directions. (Business as usual!) A reader whose day shoots by in milliseconds, who consumes information by the megabyte, and who cannot afford the luxury of climbing the learning curve with the leisurely aid of traditional narrative prose.

Here is a series for today's business reader negotiating today's learning

curve. Focusing on the personal and interpersonal skills crucial
to working successfully with customers, colleagues, subordinates, and
supervisors, the Quick-Tip Survival Guides mine and refine the nuggets of
essential business know-how: the time-tested truths, together with savvy
from the cutting-edge.

201 Ways to Say No Gracefully and Effectively is a quick read for
anyone whose business doesn't always mean saying *yes*. It's a book about
making yourself heard and getting your way—without turning off your
client, your coworker, your subordinate, or your boss.

HELPING THEM
SEE THINGS
YOUR WAY

1. Don't say yes when you mean no.

2. Do you often want to say no, but, somehow, yes always comes out instead? Make it a practice to take a deep breath and hold it for at least three beats before responding. This will interrupt your reflex *yes* response and give you the few seconds you need to think of a way to say no.

3. "No" is one of the shortest words in the English language. However, the most effective *nos* have three parts:

> First: Briefly restate the request to show that you understand and appreciate it.

> Second: Say no quickly and politely. ("Sorry, I can't.")

> Third: Express appreciation for having been asked. ("Thanks for thinking of me.")

4. The trouble with no is that it often frustrates the person on the receiving end by making him feel powerless. Counteract this by offering alternatives that empower the person to whom you are saying no: "While we can't do X, we *can* do Y or Z."

5. Say no to the *request*, not to the *person*. Do your best to separate issues from personalities. This may be as simple and subtle as saying "I cannot do X" rather than "I cannot do X *for you.*"

6. Before saying no, think about self-interest—not your self-interest, but the other guy's. Persuade him that no is not just *your* response, but the right answer for *him*. Example: You are asked to better a deadline by an unreasonable number of days. Instead of screaming bloody murder about what *you* cannot do, focus on why cutting corners is a bad idea—for *the other guy*: "I couldn't short-change your project like that. It's simply not enough time to do the caliber of job you have a right to expect."

7. One of the most effective ways to get "them" to see things your way is to make an effort to see things *their* way. Instead of saying no, compromise and negotiate a favorable solution. The classic alternative to no is quid pro quo: "If you will support me on this project, I will do everything I can to get your budget approved intact."

8. If, in a given circumstance, quid pro quo is not an appropriate alternative to no, offer a concrete alternative—preferably one that concedes and compromises without really giving up ground. A demonstration of flexibility often wins the day, whereas a flat no may bring about mutually defeating confrontation.

9. Instead of saying no, why not shift the burden of the problem to your opposite number? "How would you like me to handle this situation?" Or: "What would seem like a fair solution to you, Peter?"

10. If you decide to negotiate rather than insist on a flat no, come to the bargaining table with clear objectives, and cultivate a realistic optimism. Not only will this help to prevent you from making a costly mistake, it will show the others involved in the negotiation that you are in control.

11. To whatever degree is possible, plan any confrontations thoroughly. Know what you want, anticipate potential objections, formulate responses. This does not mean burning the word *no* into your mind, but, rather, having the relevant facts and arguments ready so that you can marshal them as required.

12. It is your right to refuse to feel guilt when you choose not to be imposed on. Take the moral and emotional equivalent of the Fifth Amendment. After saying, "No—I'm sorry—I can't do it," remain silent.

13. If possible, don't just say no and leave it at that. Practice the "feel-felt-found" approach, which helps to create a bridge of empathy and understanding that helps both of you get over the negative emotions generated by having been thwarted: "I know how you *feel* . . . I *felt* that way myself once . . . But I have *found* that . . ."

14. Say no, but not *hell, no*. It is usually better to underreact than to overreact. Emotions feed off one another. The word *no* can create powerful, usually negative, feelings. Don't stoke the fires of resentment by upping the emotional ante with a loud voice or harsh words.

NO
TO MORE WORK

15. There are three basic approaches to saying no to an assignment. You may attack the assignment itself, offering evidence that the project is flawed, unfeasible, or unnecessary. Or you may argue that, while the project is okay, you are not the best person to carry it out, either because of an absence of qualifications, a lack of experience, or because you are a resource better used elsewhere. Finally, you may simply say that you prefer not to take on the project.

16. All other things being equal, the best way to say no to an assignment is to convince your boss that you are a resource better used on a different project.

17. When you tell your boss that others are more qualified for an assignment than you are, focus attention on the alternatives you propose, not on your unsuitability.

18. Instead of rejecting an assignment out of hand, try pointing out the existence of "problems," "loose ends," "sticking points," or "questions" that "need to be resolved before proceeding." This indicates that you are still engaged with the project and gives your boss an opportunity to acknowledge the difficulties for herself. It is better than putting yourself in the uncomfortable position of criticizing her judgment.

19. When you say no to an assignment, avoid tossing the project back into your boss's lap. Instead, offer an alternative suggestion.

20. If you decline an assignment by simply claiming that you are not well suited to it, you risk creating the impression that you are walking away from responsibility. Prevent this by nominating someone else for the assignment and providing a persuasive rationale for the alternative candidate. That way, you are not simply leaving the job undone.

21. You don't have to say no to an assignment immediately. Without indicating acceptance or rejection, ask for time to review the assignment. This will allow you space to formulate alternatives.

22. Try declining an assignment by first citing a past success, then contrasting the appropriateness of that successful assignment with the unsuitability of the proposed assignment. Leave the impression that the proposed assignment is one of those *rare* instances of a project for which you are not the best choice: "As you know, I did so well with the Smith account because I know the wholesale end of the widget industry backwards and forwards. The project you're asking me to take on now calls for the same level of expertise on the retail end. I have to be honest with you: Joe is the retail expert, not me."

23. Wrap your no in a warm pair of compliments:

Ann: "I know you're not going to want to miss working on the mailing committee. Certainly, you can find time for that."

You: "That's really sweet of you to think of me like that, Ann. This year, however, I need to focus on getting out the Lindquist project, and I just don't have a spare minute. I really enjoy working with you, and I hope I'll be able to fit the committee in next time around.

24. The pile in your in-box is eight inches high. The pile in Joe Shmoe's in-box is barely an inch high. You're good at what you do. Joe isn't. Recognizing this, the boss gives you most of the work. Say no to this situation in a way that will not only bring about a fairer distribution of assignments, but will position you for greater reward and recognition rather than just more work. Discuss the situation with your boss by focusing on *his* needs and the needs of the department or company—not on your needs: "Mr. Perkins, we have a problem with the distribution of work in this department. I'm afraid that it's getting so lopsided that I can't always devote the kind of time and attention that each project deserves. I'm afraid that quality and productivity in our department will suffer." This should open the way for a frank discussion.

NO TO COLLEAGUES AND COWORKERS

25. You are invited to an office party. The last one was raucous and unpleasant, and you don't want to repeat the experience. How do you refuse without alienating your colleagues? Make a simple, non-judgmental response: "Sorry, but I won't be able to come." Your regrets should be confined to the simple, polite "sorry." No further explanation is necessary.

26. You are invited to an office party and would like to attend, but family commitments prevent your doing so. Respond with an expression of regret and a brief explanation, but avoid blaming anyone for your not being able to come. Say: "Bill, I'd really like to come, but it's Sarah's birthday, and I'm planning a special evening out with her." Avoid: "Oh, Bill, I'd *really* like to come, but Sarah would *kill* me if I did. It's her birthday. I'd be a dead man if I missed *that*."

27. Nobody likes to think of himself as a sucker, but have you ever been conned into saying yes with a line like the following? "Joe, you're the only one who can do this job right." When served a request disguised as flattery, return that serve like a tennis champ: "I'm flattered that you think so, Helen, but both Fred and Mary are qualified and available."

28. Offer an explanation rather than an excuse: "Sam, I'm sorry I can't change the location of the meeting. As you know, we had to make arrangements for the meeting well in advance and had to secure the room with a cash guarantee. We've coordinated with a dozen participants, all of whom have agreed to the meeting site. I hope you'll be able to alter your plans and that we'll see you there."

29. Expand the dimension of your *no* from yourself to the group. Bolster your response with references to the logical concept of the greatest good for the greatest number: "Clara, I was sorry to hear about the scheduling conflict that may prevent you from attending our meeting. I wish I could make a change, but all of the other participants—that's fifteen people—have agreed on nine o'clock on the 12th. You'll understand that I can't ask all of these people to change their schedules now. Is there anything else I can do to help you modify your schedule so that you might attend?"

30. Violence in the workplace? It happens every day—not out-and-out fisticuffs, but verbal jabs by bullies who won't argue the actual substance and merits of your idea, but, instead, try to beat you and the idea into the ground with a barrage of disparaging language. Say no to this by standing tall under the assault. Resist the temptation either to surrender or to rush in swinging. Instead, let the abuser land his first punches. If possible, smile blandly at him while he does this. Then step in: "I understand, Bill, that you don't approve of my plan. You've made that clear enough. That's your privilege, and you may be right. However, I feel that my plan will meet a pressing need, and after I am given a chance to explain it, we can all decide what to do with it: adapt it, change it, or just dump it."

31. A workplace is a small society, and, as in any society, alliances and enmities tend to develop. Obviously, you're better off with more positive than negative relationships. But what do you do when a coworker habitually attempts to squash your ideas and block your projects? You could say no to this behavior by leveling your big guns against the chronic critic, and maybe you'll win this or that battle—but you'll also reinforce the negative behavior and, in the long run, fight a war that either may never end or that you may even lose. Instead of attacking, then, try to convert your opponent into a new ally. Take your next idea to him *before* offering it to the group: "Karl, I'd like your opinion on something. I know that you've got a special interest in widget handling. What do you think of this . . . ?" If you can get Karl to stake an ownership interest in your idea, chances are that you'll win his support. Just be careful that he doesn't take over your work.

32. The needler—what a nuisance! This is a coworker or colleague who teases you and makes jokes at your expense. You're supposed to take it like a good sport, but the fact is that the needling is not about humor, let alone affection. It's about criticism and malice. Saying no to a needler requires shifting the object of his attack from you to something impersonal. *Needler:* "Bob, I suppose you'll move at your usual *stately* pace on formulating policy for the project." *Bob:* "Let's discuss some of that policy right now." Bob resists defending himself against an accusation of moving slowly. Instead, he deftly shifts the conversation away from himself and onto the issues.

33. When a colleague tries to take over one of your functions—horns in on your territory—you have to say no, not as a matter of pride, but of survival. It is best to avoid confrontation. Instead, make certain that you and your colleague are clear on the definitions of your responsibilities. Approach your colleague, describe the overlap you see, then work out definitions, if necessary. If at all possible, resolve the duplications between yourselves rather than appealing to higher management. Record your conclusions in memo form.

34. While it is often a good idea to state your reasons for saying no, sometimes *no* just has to mean no. Period. In these cases, don't allow yourself to be sucked into a debate. "The answer, Fred, is no. I just do not want to go down that road."

NO TO UNWANTED OVERTIME AND UNWELCOME BUSINESS TRAVEL

35. Guilt mongers delight in asking you to work overtime at the worst possible times. Before saying no to overtime, do make certain that you really don't owe it to the team or to the project. But if you don't, say no firmly and without excuse. "Marty, I just can't accommodate you on this one. I've got to get out of here by 5:30." Present this as a statement, so that there is nothing to debate or to argue about.

36. During the American Civil War, a reluctant draftee could avoid service by finding and offering a substitute to serve in his place. When you are "drafted" for overtime, accompany your no with an offer to assist in recruiting another body. "Sorry I can't stay myself, Hank, but I think Sarah is available. Do you want me to give her a call for you?"

37. Are you the one the boss *always* seeks out when overtime is called for? Say no to this situation by sitting down with your boss and working out some ground rules for overtime. Let her know that you are a team player, ambitious, ready to help out. But you've got a family life, too. "To serve you and the company more effectively, I've drawn up a schedule. These are the days when I plan to be available for overtime."

38. Salaried employees are expected to be "professionals," a dignified-sounding word that typically translates into something like *grunts-who-put-in-a-lot-more-than-five-eight-hour-days-a-week*. But what do you say when enough is enough —when you just cannot work *another* weekend? Best to keep it simple and short, without any bellyaching: "Boss, I really need some downtime this weekend. I'll give the Herbert project my full attention on Monday."

39. In saying no, don't dwell on your needs, wants, and doubts. Focus on what's "best for the department" and "most effective for the company," as well "what makes the best strategic sense for the team."

40. Before opting out of a business trip, please examine your reasons for saying no. If there is not a compelling *business* reason for refusing the trip, try to rearrange your priorities to make the trip possible. Inconvenient or not, it is part of your job.

41. If there is a pressing *business* reason for saying no to a business trip, present the case to your boss. Hand her the alternatives, and let her weigh them. (Of course, that doesn't mean you can't put your thumb on the scale!) "I agree that seeing Jacobs in Detroit is a good political move, but making the trip now would mean losing three days on the Young account—and we're looking at an April 5 deadline."

42. It is important to know, recognize, and acknowledge when you have been pushed to the limit. Don't be a martyr. Working overtime one too many hours won't do your company any good if the work shows signs of your fatigue, nor will the firm benefit from a burned-out employee. As to yourself—do you really want to suffer a breakdown? When you've been pushed to the max, you have to say no to more work: "John, I need to go home now. I'm starting to do less than a great job on this material. It certainly won't get us anywhere if I have to do half my work over again. I'll see you tomorrow morning."

NO TO SALESPEOPLE, OFFERS, AND PROPOSALS

43. If you want to say no to a sales pitch, do not invite debate. Make it clear that no means no. *Salesperson:* "I'm sure you don't have a closed mind about this." *You:* "Yes, as a matter of fact, I do. That's the end of it."

44. Junk mail you can tear up and throw away. But what about "junk calls"? First off, before you hang up on that unsolicited sales call, you might want to hear the pitch out. But once you're certain that you aren't buying what they're selling, the truly polite thing to do is to interrupt the salesperson and just say that you are not interested. You'll save yourself time, and you'll save the caller the time and energy he'd otherwise waste on a hopeless call: "No. I'm really not interested. Thanks." Then hang up.

45. Increasingly, these days, "cold calls" reach you at the office. Often, it's an investment broker of one stripe or another trying to part you from your money. If you want to put an end to such calls, politely but firmly make it clear that you do not make personal transactions during regular business hours. Advise the caller not to phone you again at the office. Feel free to break into the middle of the pitchman's spiel: "Hold on, Mr. Harris. I'm sorry to interrupt you, but I *never* do personal business during business hours. It's against my policy, and it's unfair to my employer and my clients. Please don't call me on this matter at this number again. Goodbye."

46. A pushy salesperson makes a sale—then tries to get you to add unwanted extras to your order. *Salesperson:* "Look, *everyone* orders the optional decorative trim. Let me put you down for it. It's only another $150." *You:* "Mr. Thomas, I appreciate your wanting to help me select additional options. But I do not want them. You know, my daddy used to tell me, 'Once you've made the sale, it's time to shut up.' Mr. Thomas, you've made the sale." Imply—gently and humorously, if you wish—that high-pressure tactics are endangering the deal.

47. You've solicited project proposals from a number of firms. Only one can get the contract. How do you say no to the others? You are under no obligation to give reasons for your choice; however, you may benefit from taking the time to do just that. Giving a concise reason for choosing one proposal over another is not only courteous (and therefore will create or preserve a positive relationship with a potential future supplier), it helps to educate the supplier as to how he might serve you better in months or years to come. This will benefit both of you.

48. Say no to the proposal, not to the supplier and certainly not to an individual. Keep the door ajar. "Your proposal for our water project was very impressive, Joe, and it has triggered a lot of thought here. However, your approach is just too costly, and we are going to go with a scaled-back version. But I want to thank you for a terrific effort, and I will certainly be calling on you in the future. I'm glad to have met you and to have seen what your company can do."

49. Give a second chance—*if* you want to. Offer the opportunity without excessive or misleading encouragement. Offer only *real* hope. "We've finished reviewing your proposal for supplying the equipment, and, unfortunately, what you propose is not up to spec. Obviously, we're looking at other suppliers. But there is still a month before we close out on bids. Maybe you would like to take another look at our spec sheet and submit a revised proposal by the 16th of next month?"

50. You've issued a request for proposal (RFP) and have received a wild bid from one supplier. It's so wide of the target that you've not even responded to it. Now he's on the phone. Based on the response to your RFP, you really don't want to do business with him now—or later. But in the business world, what goes around comes around, and you don't want to be unduly harsh. How do you say no? Focus on your target and on what was proposed. Avoid judgmental statements relating to capability, talent, or personality: "Frank, your proposal came in 40 percent over our target cost figures. That's a gap I couldn't see you closing. So I went with a proposal that was much closer to the target."

51. You are having trouble with a vendor whose shipments are arriving so late that manufacturing, at times, has been seriously delayed. The vendor offers excuse after excuse. How do you say no to the excuses without cutting loose a vendor who has regularly offered you very favorable prices? Translate the *I* versus *you* situation into a *we*: "I understand the problems you are facing, but we—you and I—are facing a problem, too. We need to work out a reliable schedule. Let's work together on it and agree on a new shipping plan to prevent late deliveries in the future."

52. A supervisor from another department proposes that you move to her unit. You are not interested in transferring from your department, but you certainly do not want to offend or alienate the person who has flattered you with the offer. It is best not to turn down such an offer immediately. Ask for a finite amount of time to think about it. After all, it might be a good opportunity. But even if you are quite sure that you don't want the job, asking for time to think it over shows that you honor and value the offer. When it comes time to deliver your no, express thanks, emphasize that your decision to decline the offer was a difficult one, and give a few solid reasons for your choice: "Clara, I want to thank you for your offer. I had to think long and hard about it—it's very tempting—but I believe that I can serve this organization best in the widget department. It's best for me, and it's best for the company. I am really flattered that you would make the offer, however."

NO TO CLIENTS
AND CUSTOMERS

53. A "no" goes down easier when you can give evidence of having made a "best effort" to accommodate the request. "Larry, as soon as you asked me to push the delivery date up from September 12 to August 15, I called my suppliers. I persuaded two of them to push their dates up, but two others just could not be budged. I'm afraid September 12 is the best we can do."

54. The trouble with saying no is that it may make the other person feel that you just don't care. Show that you do care, but you must nevertheless decline the request: "I wish I could expedite your order, Jim, but this is our busiest season. Not only are we back-ordered, but I've had two key people out sick. We're working on an overtime schedule as it is in order to ensure that we don't fall behind. I really wish there was something more I could do."

55. Sometimes the best way to say no is to respond to a request *with* a request—a request for patience and understanding: "I know how important it is for you to get your widget shipment delivered early, but I'm not going to be able to meet your target date. I hope that you'll be able to bear with us. We are swamped with orders that have put a burden on our own suppliers. Now, I'm going to do everything I can to expedite your order, but I must ask for your patience, understanding, and support. I expect to deliver within a week of the target."

56. Don't fall into the trap of doing a favor now just because you've done it in the past. Say no when enough is enough: "Hi, Karl. I've just received your request for revising your payment schedule. Karl, we've already revised this twice before, and I can't inflict a financial hardship on my company by changing it a third time. You can appreciate the position that would put us in."

57. *No is always less threatening if you take the time to formulate alternatives:* "John, I've just finished reviewing your request for modifications to the units you are ordering. Engineering tells me that we can't absorb the cost of the modifications on an order of this size, and I don't think that you'd be happy if I passed the costs along to you. But I have two suggestions: One is to increase the size of your order to 300 units. Now, if that won't work for you, you might consider ordering our Model A400 instead of the A350. The A400 seems to me closer to what you're actually looking for."

58. Avoid basing a no on "company policy." This makes your firm look rigid and bureaucratic, as if it values rules and routines above service and customers. Offer *reasons*—not a mindless policy— as the basis for saying no. For example, instead of responding to a request for an odd-lot order by protesting that "it is against our company policy to fill orders smaller than one gross," try: "We offer the best prices in the industry. This is possible, in large part, because we do a high-volume business, accepting orders no smaller than a gross. We just can't make the numbers work for us—or for our customers—on smaller orders. I can give you a great price on 144 units."

59. Say no, but offer a service. Your customer wants to place an order for a quantity less than the required minimum. Respond: "I'm sorry that I can't fill an order smaller than one dozen. Would you like me to modify your order accordingly?"

60. Soften the no by taking steps to avoid leaving the other person high and dry: "I sure don't like to say no to business, but I just can't offer maintenance service on Mark 6 machines anymore. I believe that Utility Corporation still services them. Perhaps you can contact them. I'll get you their phone number."

61. Giving good customer service does not always mean saying yes. Sometimes you have turn down a *request*. Just make certain that you say no to the *request*, and not to the *customer*: "I'm sorry that your Finest Dishware was damaged, Ms. Reynolds, but we cannot agree to your request for a refund. Warnings against attempting to wash the Finest Dishware in a dishwasher are clearly displayed on the box and on the bottom of the dishes themselves. What I *can* do is replace the damaged pieces at cost rather than retail. Perhaps you would find that helpful."

62. A customer asks you to make an exception to your company's exchange-only, no-refund policy. If you have any discretionary authority in the matter, consider the benefits of saying yes (a satisfied customer, who may buy more from your firm) versus the downside (a lost sale and a disgruntled ex-customer). If you cannot say yes or do not want to, then your task is to make your exchange policy look both fair and attractive: "Mr. West, we offer exchange only. That policy helps us to control our costs and allows us to give you the best possible prices. It's so important, in fact, that we state the policy clearly on each receipt. However, there is no time limit on your in-store credit. We have lots to offer, and you're welcome to come in any time. I'll record the credit, so you don't even have to remember to bring in a credit slip. When you decide on a new purchase, just identify yourself to the cashier when it's rung up."

63. It is almost always a bad idea to resort to "company policy" as your reason for saying no. However, citing more or less objective—or objective-sounding—reasons may be helpful: "The highly seasonal nature of your business puts you outside of our minimum criteria for inclusion among our credit customers" will go down easier than "I don't think your cash flow situation is a good risk for us."

NO
TO THE BOSS

64. Try to translate the pronouns "I" and "you" into "we": "*I* have reviewed the project, and have discovered that *we* have some problems."

65. Frame *no* as positively as possible by bringing up alternatives, using such phrases as "make the best use of resources," "play to my strengths," and "I'm stronger in this area." For example: "Working on project A doesn't play to my strengths. I'm much stronger in logistics, which is what project B is all about."

66. When you have to say no, avoid using words like *can't, impossible, incapable, mistaken, overloaded, ridiculous, tired, won't*, which underscore negativity and inability.

67. Some bosses are tyrants, some are bullies, others are guilt mongers, and some like to dish out the blame. All of these types can cause you grief. But when it comes to creating a chronic state of panic in the workplace, no management style can touch that of the bumbler. He's always forgetting appointments, neglecting details, waffling in the face of crisis, forgetting how to accomplish the most basic tasks. Your first impulse, naturally, is to express your impatience or even make fun of this Captain Queeg. Instead, say no to the bumbler's time-wasting ways by helping him do his job—so that you can do yours. Don't *correct* his mistakes, but focus on obtaining clarification and confirmation of instructions—*Bumbler:* "Did you ever send those papers to what's-his-name?" *You:* Let me make certain that I know what papers you mean. The Garfield account or the Holbrook project?"

68. Your boss is a tyrant, plain and simple, barking out commands like a top sergeant and really piling on the criticism. It will be difficult, but you have to try to say no to this kind of behavior calmly and without threatening the boss's self-image, which, underneath all the smoke and bluster, is probably quite fragile. Let him know that the feelings he is creating are impairing the work of the department or company: "I know how important it is to get production up, but shouting like this is affecting my ability to work efficiently. Sure, it's important for you to tell me exactly what you want me to do, but perhaps we could take some time to work out specific production targets now—work these out together."

69. It can be hard—maybe impossible—to reason with a supervisor who is also a bully. If all else fails, you might try muzzling him with the phrase "hostile work environment." This is how human resources people describe an employment situation that has become emotionally brutalizing. The phrase has been used in any number of legal actions taken against employers, in cases ranging from sexual harassment to bullying behavior. If your boss has any degree of sophistication, he will most likely recognize the phrase and understand that you understand that, as an employee, you are not powerless and obliged to take whatever is dished out to you: "Mr. Perkins, all of this hollering is not only unnecessary and belittling, it is creating a hostile work environment." One caution—do not threaten or even discuss legal action, except on the advice of your attorney.

70. The hard-driving boss can be exciting and inspiring to work for—unless she drives you into the ground with unrelenting and unreasonable demands. Achieving a livable work pace is important, and if you feel that you are being pushed too hard, tell the boss to pause in order to let you and your colleagues recoup and regroup. Remind her that even the most dedicated workers need a break. If accelerated pace is a chronic problem, you should discuss this with the rest of the staff and enlist their aid and support before talking to the boss: "Lisa, please, let's slow down for just a minute. You are running circles around us. Let's pause to work out a reasonable schedule and separate the drop-dead deadlines from those that are less crucial. We don't want to sacrifice quality for speed, and even the best of us need a break from time to time."

71. Your supervisor is on your back—almost literally. He looks over your shoulder at everything you do. You don't object to being given an assignment, but you do object to being denied the freedom to carry it out. Be gentle here, but appeal to the boss's self-interest: "David, I appreciate your hands-on approach to the assignments you give me, but, remember, you do give them to *me*. I would like to earn your confidence. I know I can increase my own productivity and the productivity of this entire department if you will consider letting up on the constant checking and directing. Give me a little space, and see what happens to our figures. I promise that you'll be pleased." Focus on departmental performance rather than on the boss's personality.

72. Your boss asks you and your spouse to dinner, but you have a previous engagement that you cannot break. This could be a very uncomfortable situation for you. Are sure that there is no way to alter your schedule? If there isn't, express your thanks and your regrets, always providing an explanation of why you cannot accept the invitation. Express your desire for another opportunity: "Mary, I really appreciate the invitation. My wife, Sarah, has been very eager to meet you. However, we are going to be out of town on the 10th for my niece's wedding, so I'm sorry that we can't accept your invitation. I hope you'll give us another opportunity."

73. Your boss has a pet project and presses you to agree with his wildly optimistic projections of revenue the enterprise will produce. You could just go along with him, but you are convinced that the project is a big mistake. The fact is that you don't have to play the part of a sheep who meekly follows the flock to slaughter. On the other hand, you should not rest with simply expressing doubts and reservations that will get you tagged as a nay sayer. Instead, offer to work on the project, but begin by demonstrating the need for a careful review of the projections: "Jack, the first thing I'd like to do is get some really detailed projections, reflecting both the best case and the worst case. I'd like to establish the most realistic foundation we can for this project."

NO
TO REQUESTS
FOR MONEY

74. For most people, the hardest *nos* are those delivered in money-related situations. You have at your disposal two tools to make this negative job a little easier: *explanation* and *hope*. When you decline a request, provide an explanation. If you realistically can, also provide hope—usually in the form of a statement of future conditions that will make it possible for you to grant the request: "Mr. Rice, you've been in business such a short time that I cannot authorize a loan. However, once you have four quarters of financials to show me, I will gladly reconsider, and if your prospects turn out to be half as promising as you say, I feel strongly that I will be able to accommodate you."

75. A long line of B-movie couples have united and parted with the phrase, "it's bigger than both of us." When you have to say no, it can be very helpful to base your response on something "bigger than both of you": "You and I are both fully aware of how volatile the market is now. Under the current market conditions, we just can't afford to risk the kind of money you're talking about. Unfortunately, it's a circumstance neither of us can control."

76. If you find it difficult to say no to a charitable request, you are not alone. Most people have trouble with this one. Before you respond, repeat to yourself: *I do not owe anyone an explanation.* Then politely decline the request: "I do not wish to contribute, but I thank you for thinking of me."

77. Sometimes you want to give an explanation for saying no to a charitable request. To coin a cliché, honesty is the best policy. At least, honesty is where you should begin. If your funds are limited, say so—but remember the magic word "discretionary": "Claire, I was quite impressed by your brochure for Help International—so impressed that I wanted to reply to you personally. Our charitable budget is exhausted for the year, so I cannot make a contribution at this time. Will you keep me in mind *early* next year, when I'll have the discretionary funds to devote to a contribution?"

78. Maybe you are a naturally generous person. And that is fine, if your disposable income runs neck-and-neck with your giving spirit. If not, you have to be selective in your charitable giving. The magic phrase here is "funds already committed": "Mr. Truman, your cause is certainly worthwhile, but my charitable funds are already committed." If you wish—but *only* if you wish—you might invite another call at a later time: "Perhaps you'd like to call me again in six months?"

79. If you are the "giving" spokesperson for your firm, you have a special responsibility to balance corporate generosity against the funds allocated for charitable purposes. What happens when you are solicited *after* your charitable budget has been spent? Be honest, and remember the phrase "funds already committed": "Karl, it's really hard to say no to a request from Community Helpers, but I'm sorry to say that I must. As you know, our company is very active in a number of community causes, but we just don't have the excess funds or the free time to devote to another organization. Our funds are already committed. I'm sorry about that, Karl, but I know that an organization as worthwhile as yours will attract many other supporters who do have available the cash and time you require."

80. There is no end of causes out in the world, and unless you are a consummately wishy-washy stump politician, you won't agree with all of them. Say no to these politely and without an argument, but you don't need to disguise your disagreement: "Ms. Washington, I have to tell you that I strongly differ with the policies of the Save-the-Viper organization, and I do not feel that I can contribute to it. I appreciate your taking the time to call me, but I ask that you do not call me again on this matter. Thanks."

81. In the name of a "good cause," office hat passers can get awfully pushy—time and time again. What if you don't want to contribute any more? Be firm and unemotional. *You:* "No, Ed." *Ed:* "Well, why not?" You don't have to give a reason, just a firm repetition: "No, not this time, Ed." If Ed is still pushy, you may want to lean on the rest of the group for support: "These office collections are getting out of hand. There should be a stated policy on giving—a reasonable policy we all agree on. Then, Ed, you wouldn't have to be in the embarrassing position of having to nag us all into making a donation."

82. You get a call from a vendor asking for early payment on a balance due. The terms are thirty days, but the vendor would like the money now and is even willing to give you a modest discount. You'd like to help out— and you wouldn't mind getting that discount—but your cash flow won't allow it. The best way to say no in this situation is to be straightforward: "Pete, I would really like to help you out, and I sure appreciate the discount offer. But my cash flow is very tight, and I just cannot accommodate you before the 30th."

83. Instead of saying no to a request for money, propose a compromise. In the case of the vendor who wants early payment, you might be able to strike a bargain. "Look, Pete, I understand that you're in a crunch. So am I. My cash flow situation doesn't permit my paying you in full now. However, I can pay half by the 10th, if that will help. And, if you take me up on it, I propose that you reduce your discount offer proportionately—say 2 percent instead of the 4 you offered."

84. A coworker asks you for a loan. You consider him a poor risk. It's a gut feeling, but a compelling one. Because your decision to say no is based on your feelings rather than on any objective evidence (the person hasn't borrowed from you in the past), you can't be very specific about providing a reason for your response. Therefore, keep it simple: "Sorry, Helen, but I'm not in a position to make any loans these days."

NO TO SUBORDINATES

85. In employer-employee or supervisor-subordinate situations, it is important to ensure that *no* does not cut off communication. Make it clear that you are responding negatively to the proposal, the request, or the idea—not to the *person* bringing you the proposal, request, or idea. "Mary, that's an interesting idea. I can't act on it at this time because of cash-flow pressures, but it's a thoughtful suggestion, which is certainly what I've come to expect from you."

86. Saying no to an employee's request for a raise is one of the hard things a manager often has to do. You can make the situation easier for both you and the employee if clear guidelines and policies, including regular annual or semi-annual performance reviews, are in place at your organization. However, even in these scenarios, a moment of truth inevitably comes. In most cases, the best course is to say no without being judgmental, hard-nosed, or apologetic. Give a straightforward reason for your response, and, if at all possible, offer rational, realistic, and clearly defined hope for the future.

87. After three months of employment, Carol Wellington wants a raise. She's doing a good job, and you don't want to discourage her, but there's no way you can afford to hand out a raise to someone who's been on the job ninety days. Offer praise and whatever promises you can honestly make: "Carol, I am really delighted with the job you've been doing for us in the three months you've been here. In that short time, you've already made a difference. But I have to emphasizes that this has been a *short* time. Ordinarily, I can't even consider a raise before one year of employment. Well, you are no ordinary employee. I would be willing to have a salary review with you in April. You'll have been here half a year then. Assuming you maintain or even improve your level of performance, I will do everything I can to get you an increase prior to the one-year mark."

88. Saying no to a request for a raise from an employee whose performance does not merit one need not be a painful experience. On the contrary, it can be a valuable and necessary wake-up call—an employee review session with a powerful sense of urgency. Whatever you say, avoid self-righteous outrage. Avoid threats. Instead, use the occasion to outline the performance conditions that will make a raise possible in the future. Turn a negative situation into a positive "educational" experience: "Pat, before we can review your compensation status, we have to review your job performance. Your present level of performance does not merit a salary increase. I need to see improvement in three areas before I will consider a raise." You then enumerate the three (or two or four or whatever) areas. Either at the present time or in a subsequent conference, you should establish clear goals for each of these areas. Close by making a bonding statement: "Pat, I am confident that, together, we can bring your performance to a level that will merit an increase—and that will improve performance for all of us here and also increase your job satisfaction."

89. A deserving employee comes to you in search of a salary increase, but you don't have the finances to give her one. What could be more negative than a bare cupboard? The truth is that even this no can be turned into a positive event—if you can show the employee that she has a very real stake in the company's performance. "Annabel, I know you deserve a raise. I could not agree with you more on this. But we have not reached a revenue level this quarter that would make a raise possible. You know that I value your contribution to this department. I am sorry I can't increase your compensation right here and now, but I feel confident that, with your continued maximum effort, we can and will reach the level of revenue necessary to give you an increase. I'm not asking you to work harder. You already work hard and smart. I'm asking you to sustain that effort and not get discouraged. Let's review this situation at the end of the next quarter."

90. Except in certain contract and union situations, no one is guaranteed regular raises. Let's say you've got a case in which the employee is doing a good job, and the company is doing well, but the employee's compensation is appropriate to his position, and, in that position, he's not going to grow. Saying no to a raise in this situation is actually an opportunity to develop an employee and bring him to the next level: "Harry, you do a good job as production coordinator. I also understand and appreciate your desire for more salary. However, you are at the top level of compensation for your position. If you want to grow financially, you're also going to have to grow in terms of responsibility. It's time for us to start to explore other opportunities within the company."

91. Salary issues present an opportunity to turn an absolute yes or no into a matter of degree. You can offer a compromise on a lesser amount or some other benefit, such as additional paid vacation. Provide a reason for the compromise: "Ted, I am very enthusiastic about your performance, and I agree that an increase is called for. However, you have been with the company only a little over a year now, and the figure you propose is inappropriately high. I'm prepared to offer a 4 percent increase. At your two-year review, we'll certainly revisit the matter."

92. Saying no to a request for promotion can be even more difficult than turning down a bid for a raise. There is a greater danger of offending pride, of injuring self-confidence, of implying that you do not appreciate the employee's accomplishments or that you simply do not believe him capable of handling greater responsibility. There is a danger of alienating a valuable team member by making him feel that he has reached a dead end and should seek opportunity elsewhere. If you value the employee, saying no to a promotion should always be accompanied by as full an explanation as you can give and, if feasible, hope for the future. If possible, the future conditions under which a promotion may be made should be outlined and defined.

93. An impatient staffer wants to move from assistant widget counter to senior widget counter. Trouble is, she's been at her job a mere four months. You have to say no, but you don't want to kill ambition and enthusiasm: "I'm really excited by your ambition and enthusiasm, as well as by your obvious commitment to this department. I see a move up to senior widget counter—and beyond—in your future. But the operative word is *future*. The earliest I could consider a promotion is in April. You have my word that we'll review your position then."

94. Few things are more frustrating for a team member—and often for the manager as well—than bumping up against a seniority policy. In general, it is best to avoid resorting to "company policy" as the basis for denying a request. Doing so can seem arbitrary and inflexible, a statement that you and the company value rules over human beings. However, such issues as seniority are often ironclad elements of company policy, and your hands may be tied. Soften the blow with an encouraging assessment: "Karen, I hope to bring you along—in salary as well as in responsibility—as quickly as I can. But, as you know, our policy is guided by seniority status. You've done a great job in the time you've been here. However, at this time, it would be unfair and inappropriate for me to put you ahead of others whose commitment and performance are comparable to yours, but who have been 'in line' longer."

95. No one knows better than a manager just how limited "authority" can be. What you are often called on to manage is situations that are beyond your direct control. An employee wants a promotion, but the firm is not filling the position at this time. How do you say no without turning off a valuable member of your team? Unite with him in *mutual* limitation: "I would like to promote you to the position, but, just now, the position is not mine to offer. The decision has been made not to fill it at this time. This situation will be reviewed, and I promise you that I'll let you know when the review takes place, and you'll be very high on the list for that position when it does open up."

96. One of the people you manage asks for a change in working hours. But a lot is going on, and you are in no position to shuffle the staff around now. You are within your rights as a manager simply to say *no* and leave the matter at that. But is this the best way to handle the issue? Whenever possible, drive your no along the road to a solution: "I've reviewed your request for a change in your working hours, Gary. Just now, we need you to be available as you are presently scheduled. I can't shake up the entire department; however, that doesn't mean that *you* can't do something about it. Why don't you discuss the matter with some of your colleagues? Perhaps one of them would be willing to work out a swap with you. I would be open to that."

97. Employees with initiative—we call them "self-starters"—are valuable to the team, but sometimes they act on their ideas without securing proper authorization. When this happens, chaos gains ground. Say no to this kind of behavior by making very clear what actions require authorization, how that authorization is to be obtained, and what the consequences are for acting without authorization: "I understand and appreciate, Ben, that you had to act quickly to get a bargain price on the computer. But our rules requiring authorization for such a purchase are clear. If we allowed unauthorized purchases like this, we'd soon be out of business. We can use the computer, and I'll authorize the purchase retroactively—this time. Next time, you'll have either to return the item yourself, or the cost of it will be taken out of your salary."

NO TO
A JOB SEEKER

98. A hopeful young face appears in your doorway: the job applicant. At the end of the interview, you conclude that this person is not right for the position. How do you break the news? Many employers remain noncommittal at the interview, telling the applicant that he will be "hearing from us" by mail. Although you may feel that this is just putting off the inevitable, a letter is in most cases the appropriate way to handle rejection. Not only is it easier on you, it conveys to the applicant the impression that you have given the matter due consideration and have not made a snap decision, which might offend the applicant and provoke challenge.

99. The interview is drawing to a close. The eager candidate is dying to know: *Do I have a chance?* The answer is no. But should you tell him now—or write the usual letter? In most cases, it is most appropriate to give the job seeker the bad news by mail. It is unwise—and not very kind—to appear to have made a snap decision by rejecting the candidate during the interview. On the other hand, it is no kindness to mislead the candidate with false praise and false hope. You may want to reply with something like this: "Mr. Young, I've enjoyed talking with you. You'll hear from us by mail in about two weeks. But, since you ask, I should tell you that, at this point, I have interviewed a number of candidates with a good deal more experience than you have. And experience is the principal thing I'm looking for."

100. You are seriously interested in the candidate you are interviewing. Then it becomes clear that her salary expectations are way out of line with what you are prepared to offer. How do you say no to the money without losing a good prospect? The hard fact is that, depending on how important salary is to this candidate, you may just lose her. Certainly, you should make no false or misleading promises. At best, this will lead to disappointment and will lay a weak foundation for a good working relationship. At worst, false promises may become grounds for a costly legal dispute. Instead, try to demonstrate how the compensation you propose is appropriate for the position, and try to "sell" the candidate on the position's non-monetary benefits. If the prospect of advancement is real, mention it. "Ms. Rufus, the figure you mentioned is not possible for this position. The salary range is from $XX,XXX to $XX,XXX. This is well within the standard for the industry—and, at its upper end, better than most firms offer for a similar position. It is a position that gives a self-starter like yourself a lot of room for creativity. It is a high-visibility position, which means that it is a very good place from which to advance. I know that salary is important, but the considerations I've just mentioned are the things that differentiate a career from a job."

101. In most cases, you do not owe a job applicant a long explanation for having turned him down. If an application was sent in unsolicited, you may simply reply (if you reply at all) that "no suitable position is currently available":

> "Thank you for sending your résumé and letter. At this time, no suitable position is open at Acme Widgets. We appreciate your interest in Acme Widgets."

If you wish—but only if you really do wish to encourage the applicant—you may remark that the letter and résumé are "impressive." Do not feel obliged to say this, however, if the applicant clearly has no hope of ever finding a job at Acme Widgets. Being polite is not worth building up false hope.

102. If the skills of the job applicant are not suitable to the position, write a simple letter stating this fact. And do state it as a fact, rather than as an opinion. Don't invite dispute:

"Thank you for your application for the position of service technician with Acme Widgets.

"After a careful review of your application, our selection committee has determined that your experience and skills, while impressive, do not suit the position. We cannot pursue your application further.

"Acme Widgets wishes you the best of luck in securing a position appropriate to your skills."

103. If having to say no to an applicant is a matter of inadequate experience rather than unsuitable skills, say so. Express the rejection in terms that avoid dispute. Here is a letter to a recent college graduate, who has no sales experience—let alone the "five years" the position calls for:

Thank you for applying to Acme Widgets for the position of sales manager.

"Your educational background is highly impressive, but the position of sales manager demands at least five years of sales experience. We cannot, therefore, pursue your application further.

"Acme wishes you the best of luck in finding a position appropriate to your potential and interests."

104. A valued client asks you to "find a job" in your organization for a son or daughter. The problem is that the client's offspring is not only unqualified for anything you have to offer, but terminally inept. You can't allow your firm to be sandbagged by a dud, but you don't want to alienate the client, either. By all means, interview the young person. Show that you take the client's request seriously. Then, in talking to the client, concentrate on such manifestly objective issues as education and experience, rather than subjective items such as talent, intelligence, and character: "Your kid's sharp, no doubt about that, but I need someone with at least five years of experience in widget sales. I'll keep him in mind if something opens up at an entry level, but I'm sure he'll be well placed somewhere else by then."

105. "Increasingly these days, savvy job hunters are calling managers to request "informational interviews." These are not job interviews per se, but an effort to become acquainted with the company, to scope out opportunities there, and to make contact with the people who do the hiring. Should you get such a call, consider resisting the knee-jerk impulse to decline a meeting on the grounds of having no job to offer. If the caller has enough smarts to approach the job-hunting process through informational interviewing, chances are he or she is the kind of employee you want in your organization. However, if you absolutely do not have the time or the inclination to set up a meeting, you may still want to say no in a way that leaves the door ever so slightly ajar: "Ms. Perkins, I won't have time to see you in the near future, and we don't have any positions open at present. However, I certainly appreciate your interest in us, and I admire your initiative. I would like to keep your phone number on file. If our needs change here, I'll call you."

106. "I know I've called you before—several times—and you've said that you have nothing available, but I just want you to know that I'm eager to learn, and I would be your hardest worker. I *really, really, really* need a job." Sooner or later, if your position involves hiring, you'll find yourself dogged by a persistent job seeker. If you don't have a secretary or executive assistant who can screen his calls, you finally have to come up with a way to say no once and for all: "Mr. Smith, I've told you repeatedly that it is a waste of your time and mine for you to call regarding employment here. We hire people with a minimum of five years of experience in the field. Period. Furthermore, we value employees who can follow and execute instructions. I've asked you not to make further inquiries here. Those were my instructions to you. They are my instructions today. I wish you good luck in finding a suitable position—elsewhere."

NO TO INAPPROPRIATE LANGUAGE OR BEHAVIOR

107. Questions that pry into your personal life are inappropriate in the workplace. When idle curiosity prompts a question you don't want to answer, respond politely but firmly: "That's one I never answer." Or: "I prefer not to say." Or: "I'm sure we'd both be more comfortable avoiding personal questions like that."

108. If you are asked a question that is uncomfortably personal or prying, don't show offense. Try lightening up with a flip response. For example, sooner or later, someone will try to find out how old you are. If you want to answer, fine. If not, how about a humorous response that blows the question off good naturedly? Try: "I was born some time after the Golden Age of Television."

109. It is not appropriate for a potential employer, your current employer, or anyone else at work to ask you about your religious beliefs. Usually, the question will be posed like this: "Do you go to church?" or "What church do you attend?" rather than a straightforward "What are your religious beliefs?" If you do not wish to respond, simply say, "I think that's a personal matter and not relevant to the job."

110. Gossip and rumors are the common cold of the workplace. There is no cure, but there are remedies. If you are the victim of gossip, the way to say no to being a target is to confront the gossip head on. This does not mean being combative, but it does require that you ask pointed questions: "Why don't we talk about your feelings on this matter?" Avoid public confrontations. A private meeting—perhaps over lunch—is better. If the gossiper denies having been responsible for a rumor, you can still deflate the gossip. *You:* "I hear that you have been saying such-and-such about me." *Gossip:* "Me? No. Who told you that? How could that be? No, that's not true at all." *You:* "Good. I'm relieved you didn't say those things. Now I'll stop hearing that on the grapevine."

111. Another way to prune the office grapevine is to *make use of* the grapevine yourself. If you can identify the source of a rumor, have a private meeting with him. Don't scold. Just explain your point of view. Soon, the rumor monger will start spreading *your* side of the story.

112. Do you want to get tough on gossip? If you are in a position of authority, do two things: Set an example by refusing to pass on rumors yourself, and let your subordinates know that spreading rumors is destructive, not only to the company, but to careers. A person could gossip himself right out of a job.

113. Your boss gets too close—uncomfortably close—to you. He makes a pass. You don't want to be treated this way, but you don't want to put your job in jeopardy, either. If you ever feel pressured into accepting unwanted sexual advances from anyone at the workplace, it is your right to say no. Make it a clear, calm, and firm no, a no that cannot be misconstrued as a flirtatious "yes" or "maybe." "Mr. Hendricks, you are getting too close to me. It makes me uncomfortable, and it is inappropriate." If the attentions persist, be certain to use some form of the word *harassment*. Most bosses will hear the word as a synonym for *lawsuit*: "Mr. Hendricks, I do *not* want to be harassed in this way." If the situation persists, file a complaint with corporate human resources and with your boss's superior. If necessary, seek legal counsel. Sexual harassment in the workplace is destructive, intolerable, and wholly unacceptable.

114. A colleague makes a sexually offensive joke. Should you object to it? This is a personal decision. If the joke is an isolated incident, perhaps it is best just to ignore it. But if you are offended by a repeated pattern of off-color humor, meet with the misguided comedian privately: "Ted, I've been meaning to talk to you about your off-color humor. I have to tell you, quite frankly, that your jokes make me very uncomfortable. I also don't think that they are appropriate in the workplace. But, most of all, they hurt me. I'd appreciate it if you'd either keep off-color humor to yourself or share it with others when I'm not around."

115. Within your hearing, a coworker makes a racially or ethnically barbed remark that you find personally offensive. You can let it pass, of course, but prejudice is much like a cancer. It is a sickness ignored at our peril. If you feel strongly enough about it, ask the offender for a moment to speak *privately*, and, *in private*, explain to her that her remarks hurt you, make you feel bad, make you feel uncomfortable, make you feel angry. Tell her that such remarks undermine the integrity and cohesiveness of the team and threaten the entire organization, which, after all, is built on trust, cooperation, and mutual respect. Do not demand an apology. But, be assured, you will receive one.

116. The sniper attacks from cover. She doesn't offer straightforward criticism, but sly comments, belittling innuendo, and malicious insinuation, often cloaked in humor. Typically, the sniper chooses more than one target, so you are probably not alone. If this is the case, discuss the problem with the sniper's other victims and enlist their aid in bringing her out into the open. At the next meeting where the sniper attacks, call her out. *Sniper:* "Don't give up, Steve. Maybe you'll get it right—one fine day." *Steve:* "Was that meant as a criticism of something I'm doing?" Now, say to the group: "Help me out here. Did you hear what I heard?" The others then address the sniper: "Mary, could you make your criticism clear?" "I don't understand what you are implying." "Could you be clearer about whatever problems you see here?" She'll think twice before taking another shot at you—or anyone else.

117. Chronic grumbling is inappropriate and destructive behavior. Saying no to it requires a combination of firmness and empathy. *Grumbler:* "I really can't stand it here. There is no room for creativity. Management just plain sucks." A helpful reply is non-judgmental, calm, and caring. Nevertheless, its immediate purpose is to put an end to talk that can destroy morale: "Gary, I hate to see you so unhappy. We all appreciate the work you do. It's important to the organization. Very important. Now, let's talk and see if we can sort out some of the problems you're encountering."

118. You want your staff to tell you when something is wrong, and if that means complaining about a coworker, so be it. However, when such complaining becomes habitual—when one of your staff becomes a self-appointed snitch—you need to say no to such destructive behavior. It can undermine a team and tear an office apart. The most effective way to checkmate a snitch is to send her back to the target of her complaint. *You:* "Why don't you and Nate get together for an informal meeting—maybe over lunch—and work this problem out together?" *Snitch:* "You know that won't work." *You:* "Well, let's do this. I will tell Nate what you've told me—confront him—and give him the opportunity to respond." *Snitch:* "Uh, no. That would be a bad idea." *You:* "Another alternative is for me to set up a meeting among the three of us to work this out." *Snitch:* "No, no." *You:* "Okay, look, why don't you just get back to me when you want to get together with Nate on this problem. We'll figure out how to do it." You probably won't hear from the snitch again.

NO TO NUISANCES

119. You don't *owe* anyone an explanation when you refuse to be imposed on. In these cases, "Sorry, I can't" is an appropriate response.

120. "Can you look at my report now? I'm not through with it. But I *need* you to look at it. Can you just make some time *now*?" Maybe you can. Maybe you can't. Maybe this is the twelfth time Bill has asked you to check on the progress of his report. The fact is that you have the right—and the need—to control your own time. If you spend your day reacting to what others need, well, pretty soon it's no longer *your* day at all. Take charge, calmly, but firmly—confidently, but without betraying your irritation: "Bill, I can look at your report this afternoon. Please put it on my desk by four." You do not owe Bill any further explanation.

121. It is natural to deal with a fire by dumping a bucket of water on it. But maybe you recall from high school chemistry that, when some substances burn, the application of water just intensifies the flames. Saying no to a nuisance can be like trying to douse burning phosphorous with H_2O. It will just feed the flames. Instead, put him out positively: "I'll be happy to take care of that for you. Let's schedule another call—say, for Friday?"

122.   One thing is certain about a nuisance: he will strike at the worst possible time. Don't explode. Be firm—but offer the promise of attention: "I can't discuss this now, but I do know how important this is to you. I can review the situation with you on Thursday—say, 11 o'clock."

123.   The nay-sayer, who habitually tries to smother every new idea with a wet blanket, can be a mere nuisance or a genuine menace, threatening to choke all the innovative spirit out of a team, a department, or a company. Don't try to convert a nay-sayer into an optimistic enthusiast. It won't happen. As usual, the most effective way of coping with a destructive personality type is to bypass *personality* altogether and deal instead with *issues. Nay-Sayer:* "Look, it just won't work. I know all about this market. An item like this will never be accepted." *You:* "We do have to be cautious, of course, but this idea looks like it has legs. Let's take it to the next step and see how it stacks up against our past experience. After all, we do need to be more competitive in the widget category."

124. Say no with your feet. If you find yourself in the company of negative nuisances—nay-sayers and chronic critics—walk away from them. Try instead to associate with vital, positive people.

125. Kibitzers—they're the folks who stroll by your office when you're in the middle of some difficult project and tell you (nobody asked them, of course) what you're doing wrong. The object is to brush off the kibitzer without being obviously impolite: "Thanks for your opinion, but I've planned this approach from the beginning, and I can't change horses in midstream." Then deliberately break eye contact, look down at your work, and start typing or writing. The kibitzer should take his cue and leave.

126. Bill, in the cubicle next to yours, never seems to have his own supplies. He's always "borrowing" pencils, paper, paper clips—you name it. It has started to get annoying. The next time he asks you for something, try this: "Bill, I'm not going to *lend* you my paper clips. I'm going to *give* you three—count 'em, three—and I'm going to sit down with you right now and show you how to order supplies for yourself. It's a very simple form . . . ."

127. At first it was flattering. Harriet would bring her work to you, tell you how much she valued your opinion, then ask you to read and "edit" what she had done. Now it's become a habit and a nuisance. You can't afford to spend so much time poring over somebody else's work! Better say no now, before your resentment boils over: "Harriet, I'm always flattered when you ask me to look over what you've done. But I don't think you need my input on your work anymore. If you really get stuck on something, sure, come and see me. But you're doing fine on your own. Besides, my taking the time to look over your material is really starting to slow the both of us down."

NO TO UNREASONABLE DEMANDS

128. When the Lord said "thou shalt not," His words had the strength of a commandment. In some situations, you may likewise be able to put the no in the mouth of an anonymous and powerful third party. "Mr. Thomas, I would *like* to give you another extension on your loan payment, but our attorneys will not permit that."

129. One measure of having achieved adulthood is learning to live with the consequences of one's actions. Unfortunately, not everyone over age twenty-one has reached this level. A customer places an order for Product X, you fill it, then the customer calls insisting on a refund because she's decided she *really* wants Product Y: "Ms. Hopkins, I'm sorry that your husband isn't pleased with the color of the carpeting you ordered and we installed. But that *is* the carpeting you ordered and accepted. While I can't offer you a refund, I can give you an excellent price on new carpeting, and I'll remove—at no cost—the carpeting we installed. On the other hand, given a little time, you may succeed in convincing your husband that you've purchased the best carpeting in the business, and in a very attractive color, too."

130. Perks. We all hear about them. We all want them. But sometimes you have to say no. Try to deliver this response as an assessment of real need versus cost. Avoid the appearance of an arbitrary no, and, if possible, avoid such one-dimensional responses as "it's not in our budget." Here's a better reply: "Helen, I've thought about your request for a new computer. At this time, I'm not prepared to authorize the purchase of one. You do light-duty word processing and little or no accounting work. In view of that, I can't justify the overhead expense. My judgment is that the machine you have is adequate to the requirements of your job."

131. More perks. "Glenn, you make a persuasive argument for a private office. There's no denying that it would be quieter for you. But I don't have the facilities to offer you one, and, besides, your position does not require client conferences or other private meetings. Beyond this, other folks at your level do not have private offices in this organization. I know this isn't what you wanted to hear, but I hope that, as I've explained the circumstances, you'll appreciate that the decision is an appropriate one."

132. A customer telephones you to "bend the rules." Here's what he wants: "I have one of your technicians out here doing routine maintenance on my widget. He tells me that it is time to have the safety override switch replaced. Look, I just want him to remove the device. It doesn't help me. I'll take the responsibility. But he won't do it." Where safety is concerned, there is no "bending" rules. You must say no. But that does not mean adopting a holier-than-thou attitude. Instead, educate the customer, stressing that the safety device is integral to the machinery and that it is for the protection of the user: "Our technician won't remove it because doing so would endanger you and anyone else who uses the machine. Furthermore, if we did simply remove the device, the interlocking mechanism would prevent the unit from operating. It would require an extensive modification to make that machine work without the safety device. And that wouldn't be cheap."

133. A customer brings in a product for warranty repair. It is apparent that a third-party modification has been made that voids the warranty. How do you say no when the customer expects service? Avoid preaching or scolding. Instead, announce the problem quickly, then focus the customer away from what you cannot do for him and direct her attention instead to what you can do: "Ms. Smith, the unit you returned to us for warranty repair was modified in a way that voids the warranty." The customer may protest and express disbelief. Avoid accusing the *customer* of having made the modification. Address the issue, not the customer. "Yes, a framiss bypass was added, which caused premature failure of the widget. However, I have a suggestion that I believe will be helpful. I can offer you out-of-warranty repair even on this modified unit. Shall I explain how that works and what it will cost?"

134. Of the many unreasonable demands you fend off on a daily basis, perhaps the most common is the frenzied demand for immediate action or information. Usually, you don't need to say no to this kind of demand so much as you simply need to buy time—without, however, appearing as if you are stalling or being evasive. Confronted by a telephone question you can't immediately handle, try one of these: "My other phone is ringing. I'll get right back to you," "I have someone on the other line. May I call you back?" "I have someone in my office just now. Let me wrap it up here, and I'll call you back," "Do you mind waiting a moment while I check that for you?"

135. Another way to answer an unreasonable demand for an immediate response is just to say no: "You caught me short on that one. I need time to get the information you want." Or: "I'm in the middle of a major meeting. I don't want to give your concerns short shrift. May I call you back?"

136. People are always trying to take your time. By all means, share your time, but don't let anyone take it. *Client:* "Look, I need an answer to this right away." *You:* "I know how important this is to you, and I want to give it my full attention, so I am going to check into it now and get back to you on Wednesday."

137. Face it: Your client expects you to be an instant expert on whatever happens to concern him at the moment. This is an unreasonable demand, all right, but it is one to which you should say no without *appearing* to say no: "I do have some ideas about that. Can I get back to you with them on Friday?"

138. Your boss has hired an outside consultant who high-handedly demands that you change your invoicing procedure. Your first impulse is to be confrontational and just say no. Instead, however, you take a deep breath and adopt a pacifying approach to buy time: "I'll give what you say some serious thought." But the consultant is insistent: "This kind of invoicing will just *have* to go." Day by day, he provokes you, always turning the screw. Nevertheless, keep pacifying: "I need some time to review this, so that we can see how to approach it." If this fails to get the "expert" off your back, try proposing an alternative or compromise: "This is what I believe would work for us . . ." Finally, if necessary, risk confrontation: "I understand what you are showing us, but in our situation, your system is just not appropriate."

NO TO
TIME WASTERS

139. One of your coworkers likes to drop by your desk for impromptu chats—nothing about work, of course, but just passing the time of day. The time of your day. Never underestimate the value of small talk in business. It can cement bonds between you and your colleagues, can help forge a team spirit, and generally maintain a high level of morale. However, sometimes enough is enough, and it's time to get down to the task at hand. Terminate time wasting by politely and specifically pointing out what you have to do. Avoid saying, "Tom, I've got work to do." Instead, try: "Tom, you'll have to excuse me, but the Gilbert report has got to get done by the eleven o'clock meeting." If you don't have a pressing task, cite one that is as specific as possible: "Tom, I'm just settling down to catching up on my mail. Let's talk later."

140. You are asked to participate on a busy-work committee. You can't afford to alienate the chairperson, but you also can't afford to get bogged down in a waste of time. Because you value the person making the request, you owe him an explanation for saying no. The only acceptable explanation in this case is one that demonstrates beyond dispute that, right now, *for the good of the company*, your time and effort are better invested in projects other than this committee. "Max, I'm afraid this opportunity comes at a really bad time for me. I have got to devote 100 percent effort to Project X. You know what's riding on that. I'll be happy to help you find somebody else to serve on the committee."

141. It's not very healthy to think of members of your family as time wasters, but if your children or spouse makes it a habit to call you at work with matters that could wait for a more appropriate time, you need to say no. Hold a "family meeting" and make your preferences clear. One reasonable alternative to barring calls altogether ("I *told* you *never* to call me here!") is to set up a special time of day when calls from the family are welcome. You might also set up a regular time when you will call home to say hello, check in, and see how things are going. Of course, make it clear—especially to kids—that you can be reached any time in an emergency, but be certain that all family members understand just what an emergency is and is not.

142. Juggling family business and just plain business can be difficult. So why not try *balancing* the two instead of juggling them? When that call comes in from spouse or child while you are trying to get one load of papers off your desk to make way for another, promise that you will devote full time to the issue when you get home, but that you cannot now give it the time and attention it deserves: "Dear, I want to discuss this with you when I get home. I want to give it my undivided attention. Right now, I have to finish the Jones account work."

143. No matter how many or how few customers or clients you have, each one, deep down, thinks she is your *only* customer—or, at least, the only one that really matters. It is difficult to say no to a client phone call that goes on and on, but, in order to serve the other people who depend on you, you must be able to break away from the conversation—gracefully. If possible, say no to the endless phone call by implying that you are hanging up in order to do what the client is paying you for: "George, I'm going to cut this short to get started on the research you need." Whatever you say, make certain that it includes the pronoun *you*.

144. A customer or even a coworker calls you to get some information . . . then wants to chat. Trouble is, you've got work to do. How do you say no to this demand on your time without alienating someone who just wants to be friendly? Enlist their help. "Pat, I've got a deadline bearing down on me. Can you help me to get off this phone?" Try it. It works.

145. In a mad rush to create more cost-effective office environments, managers and planners have developed the open-office layout, with its warrens of cubicles rather than traditional four-walled offices with doors. The absence of doors and of floor-to-ceiling walls invites a phenomenon that is hardly cost effective: continual conversation. In today's typical office, it has become increasingly imperative to say no to unwanted conversation—without, however, offending folks with whom you work every day. But maybe you don't have to *say* anything: Try arranging your work station so that you can turn your chair away from passing people. Don't let them even catch your eye.

146. If non-verbal cues fail to discourage unwanted conversation, you'll have to be forthright, even to the point of cutting someone off in mid sentence: "Patricia, you'll have to excuse me. I'd like to talk, but I have an *impossible* deadline to meet." Keep it terse and unemotional. Avoid the holier-than-thou approach ("*Some* of us have work to do here!").

147. Seasoned business professionals never say that their phone call has been put on hold. With justifiable impatience, they talk about being put on "ignore." It is better to avoid this situation altogether by hanging up rather than hanging on. *You:* "What's the status of the Baker account, George?" *George:* "I'll look that up. Please hold on while . . ." *You, interrupting:* "George, please give me a call back as soon as you've found the information. Thanks. Bye." Hangs up.

148. You need that second cup of coffee. Two or three of your friends gather in the break room as you pour yourself a cup. The conversation begins. And goes on. And on. Break away with a *simple* and *non-judgmental* line: "I've got to get back to the Smith project." Or: "Wow! I've got an 11 o'clock meeting to prepare."

149. One of your subordinates is—let's not pull punches here—a deadbeat, a loafer. It's time to shake him up—or shake him out. You cannot afford nonproductivity in your department: "Jack, you've left early *every* day this week. Look, we all have to skip out once in a while, but the hours you are keeping are unacceptable. Jack, please consider this a warning. The next time you leave before 5:30, you *must* report to me. If you don't, I will take action."

150. You've always been a liberal, informal supervisor. But, lately, the in-office socializing has gotten out of control. It's time to set limits: "Henry, Sarah, Bill, I've asked you to meet with me because we're having a productivity problem in this office. I want for us all to be happy and satisfied here, but this is a place of business. The socializing and the chit-chat have been getting in the way of our work. We can't tolerate it any longer. Please, let's confine socializing to the break room."

151. What? A perfectionist can be a *time waster*? When a colleague's or subordinate's perfectionism gets in the way of her finishing a job, time is being lost, and productivity suffers. Help the perfectionist balance her quest for absolute excellence (on the one hand) with the immediate demands of a commercial enterprise (on the other): "Helen, what I need now doesn't have to be perfect. A reasonable draft will do very well. I understand that the draft you have is not all that you want it to be. But you'll have time to polish the work later, and we need to move the project ahead *now*."

152. Whenever you are tempted to waste time or to heed the advice of people who waste time, say no to that choice by recalling the old Spanish adage: "Tomorrow is the busiest day of the week."

NO TO OFFICE BULLIES

153. Bullies are accustomed to getting unquestioning compliance and to rolling right on over defiance. Say no these tactics by offering the bully neither compliance nor defiance. Deflate the windbag by making him think. For example: You are told in no uncertain terms that a task has to be completed days ahead of schedule. You point out that this is impossible—if a quality job is to be done. Predictably, the bully takes a deep breath and starts to huff and to puff. Before he blows your house down, frame your *no* this way: "Bill, what's your objection to doing a quality job?"

154. The bully's goal—whether he's your boss, a client, or a coworker— is to make you feel like a child, a little person incapable of standing up for himself. In order to say no to a bully, you must first say no to this self-image. One good way is to begin by emotionally cutting the bully down to size. Do his socks always match? If not, focus your attention on that inadequacy. Of course, you can't rely on a bully's always having two colors of hosiery, so find the equivalent of the mismatched socks: the habitual misuse of a word, a disagreeable personal odor, a tendency to drool—any petty detail that humanizes and humbles the bully in your eyes.

155. While you are thinking about the bully's foibles, find something to compliment him on. This may stick in your throat because it tastes too much like sucking up. Actually, it's manipulation—and *you're* doing the manipulating. Make the bully feel good about something relatively neutral: the choice of necktie, the color of his jacket. Enjoy what it feels like to be thinking about the bully in a most unflattering light even as you compliment him. It will give you a surprisingly heady feeling of power. Don't just try it, *practice* it. The technique gets more effective the more often you use it.

156. Another method of saying no to a bully is to go out of your way to *empower* him. That's right. In essence, a bully feels powerless and typically substitutes bluster for genuine confidence. Try addressing the bully's insecurity in a positive way. Consciously shift responsibility to him by asking his advice on various matters. Make it clear that he is someone you admire and from whom you have much to learn. This is an especially powerful technique when it is manipulatively combined with focusing on the bully's weak points—from mismatched socks to mistaken thought processes.

157. It's not always bosses who do the bullying. High-handed subordinates also specialize in intimidation that cuts across corporate ranks. Say no to the subordinate intimidator by establishing—or re-establishing—rules and enforcing them. *Subordinate:* "I want to get my project finished, so I'm not going to have the log sheets in until Tuesday." *You:* "That isn't acceptable. The rule is that log sheets come in on Friday. If they don't, *everyone's* schedule is torpedoed. I obey the rule, and I expect you to do the same."

158. Some work situations involve your doing part of a job, then passing it on to someone else. A certain species of bully intimidates not by criticizing your part of the job, but by revising or redoing it without even bothering to consult you. Such behavior undermines your authority and credibility—and takes the results of your work out of your hands. Talk to the offender about it, but begin on a positive note, *thanking* him for what he's done. "John, I want to thank you for going over my work, but it's not fair for you to have to take the time to do that. In addition, it is important that I retain control over what I do. That means that I have to go over the changes *you've* made. So, next time, why don't you just review with me any questions you might have. It will save both of us a lot of time."

159. A frontal assault on your competence is a favorite bullying technique. We all have insecurities, of course, and some of us are more vulnerable to this kind of attack than others. But even if you do have some doubts about your work, this is not the time to let yourself get rattled. Neither cowering before the bully nor blowing up at her is an effective response. Instead, accept the criticism politely, as if it had been offered in a helpful spirit (it wasn't!), then redirect the conversation away from personalities and toward issues. You may have to be persistent, but this approach will tend to take the wind out of the bully's sails: *Bully:* "Larry, I just don't think you know how to direct this operation." *You:* "I would appreciate any help or suggestions you might be willing to offer, Jane. Just what do you see wrong here that I could do differently?" Maybe you'll actually get some concrete—and even helpful—suggestions. More likely, if the bully doesn't fold at this point, she'll try to renew the attack: "It's *you*. I don't think you've got the experience to pull this off—not based on what I've seen. I have to be frank about it." *You:* "I appreciate your frankness, but things seem to me to be going quite well. Just where do you see room for improvement or for taking a different approach—and why? It would help me to know." Persist. This is a war of attrition, in which your courtesy and appeal to rationality will outlast the bully's reserves of negative emotion.

160. A bully bulls his way into situations, deliberately screening out you and what you have to say. Typically, there is no such thing as a *conversation* with a bully. He'll assume both sides of the discourse by putting words into your mouth: "What Alice means to say is . . . " Or: "Alice never lets anybody do that. Isn't that right, Alice?" Or: "You *can't* mean that, Alice." The only way to say no to letting a bully steal your voice is to be persistent and allow him get away with nothing. Block him at every turn: "No, Bill, that's not what I said." "Bill, you didn't hear what I said." "Bill, I've never said that." "I would never put it that way." "Bill, I have never spoken to you about my feelings on that issue."

161. Bullies bellow. They snort and roar. This can be quite intimidating—if you choose to let it be. But it's pretty difficult to sustain a bellowing session if there is no one around to listen. You do not have to accept verbal abuse. Once the bully begins to bellow, wait for a lull, then reply as softly and as calmly as you can: "Bill, I can't outshout you, and a shouting match wouldn't be very productive anyway. I'm going back to my office (or out to the break room, or somewhere away from Bill). Let's get back together when we can have a calm, civil conversation."

162. A bully seldom argues the merits of an issue. Instead, her favorite rhetorical technique is called "poisoning the well." It works like this. Let's say three opinions— A, B, or C—are possible concerning a certain issue. The bully will not debate the relative merits of each, but will weigh in with a statement like this: "Anyone who believes A or B has rocks in their head. You have to be crazy to believe A or B. Or just plain stupid." So far as A and B are concerned, the well is poisoned—if, that is, you accept the bully's statements. But why accept them? Reply: "I'm not so sure, Lauren. Let's examine all three alternatives." Or: "That's making quite an assumption, Lauren. It seems to me that A and B have some merits worth examining."

163. A bull has horns, and another argumentative technique favored by the bully is putting you on the horns of a dilemma, forcing you to take an either/or, yes/no, black/white stand on an issue: "Look, either you are for the project or against it." Sitting on the pointy horns of a dilemma is quite uncomfortable, so why agree to do it? Reply: "Pete, I don't agree. I'm not in favor of either project, but Project A could be modified in a way that would win me over. Let's discuss it."

164. Yet another weapon in the bully's rhetorical arsenal is the misused analogy: "We need to be unanimous on this point. Doubt is like a cancer. It's got to be cut out and killed wherever you find it." Who can argue with that? Nobody thinks cancer is a good thing. But is doubt really like such a disease? The bully's saying it is doesn't make it so. Beware of falling into the analogy trap. "Pete, honest doubt is *nothing* like cancer. I agree that we need to get a consensus on this project. But that doesn't mean we have to march in lockstep. Let's listen to the doubters and weigh what they have to say. We should welcome their input."

NO TO IMPOSSIBLE ASSIGNMENTS

165. Do not protest the unworkability of an assignment just to get out of doing it. However, if you are convinced that a project is doomed, present your well-reasoned doubts to your boss: "I've reviewed the assignment, and a number of very sticky points have come up. We'd better discuss these before taking action."

166. Is the assignment impossible or is it just that expectations concerning the outcome are unreasonable? Sort this out before you say no to the assignment, then analyze the assignment and advise your boss or client of the probable outcome. "Harry, I don't want you to have unrealistic expectations about the study you're asking me to undertake. It will give us some idea of consumer preference, but it will not accurately predict our market share. Here's why . . . "

167.   Maybe you are afraid of the consequences of saying no to an impossible assignment. After all, as Alfred, Lord Tennyson wrote in "The Charge of the Light Brigade," "Ours not to reason why." But you'd better read the next line of that poem: "Ours but to do and die." *And die?* Is such an outcome going to benefit you or your organization? It may be difficult to say no to an impossible assignment, but the consequences of not saying no may well be worse for everybody concerned. The solution is not simply to say no, but to explain your negative response. Reason it out with your boss or client.

168.   Learn the art of saying no to an assignment without attacking the competence or authority of the person who issued the assignment. The first step is to resist the impulse to reject the assignment out-of-hand. Walk away with it, think about it, evaluate its feasibility. If it really does look impossible, return to the person who made the assignment and present a clear and cogent evaluation. In this way, you are focusing on issues rather than the abilities of the person who gave you the task. You might present your evaluation this way: "As you see, Frank, there are some real problems with the project. Maybe we can work together to modify it."

169. Shift the burden onto the taskmaster. Presented with an impossible assignment, take it away, study it, then return: "Cheryl, how would *you* approach this?" Maybe you'll learn something. Or maybe Cheryl will realize that what she's asked you to do can't be done.

170. The old adage of business—the customer is always right—is a good place to start from, but it's not always the best place to end up at. If your client assigns you an impossible task, don't humor him. Your job is to *serve* the customer, and it is no service to do something you know won't work—even if it's what the customer wants. Say no by *educating* the customer: "Mr. Thomas, if I take that approach, you're going to end up with something that just won't do what you want it to do. Here's why . . . " Then propose an alternative.

171. Sometimes the impossible assignment is answering a question that puts you in an impossible position. Two of your colleagues are having an intense argument. One of them demands that you take sides: "Where do you stand on this?" You certainly don't want to be caught in the middle, but emotions are running so high that you don't want to appear to evade the question, either. In a case like this, try answering an impossible question with another question: "Well, Joe, Bill, what do both of *you* think the most effective way of handling this situation would be? Instead of hollering at each other, what issues should the two of you be trying to resolve?"

NO
TO BAD IDEAS

172. Interesting word, *brainchild*. It should tell you just how strongly some people feel about their ideas. Say no to an idea, and you run the risk of spurning someone's intellectual flesh and blood. Frame your *no* so that it *turns down* but does not *tear down* the idea. "That's a very thoughtful response, and if X and Y weren't factors here, I think it would work just great. However, in this particular situation, we still have to keep looking for a solution."

173. Your boss has an idea. Your boss has a *bad* idea. Let's assume that you are not in a position to respond to it with something like, "If I stayed up all night, I couldn't come up with a worse idea." So how do you dodge this dud? If possible, withhold judgment on the idea. Instead, redirect the boss's energy to day-to-day reality: "Do you want me to put the Youngblood project on the back burner? We're facing a fairly critical deadline, but if you think it's important . . . " Transmit to your boss the following message: *If I pursue your dream, everything else we do will have to be rescheduled, delayed, or sacrificed.*

174. Never tell a person in power that you have no time to act on her idea. Instead, focus on the nitty-gritty things that will have to be done in order to act on the idea: the other projects that will have to be rescheduled, the meetings that will have to be arranged and rearranged, the budget requests that will have to filled out. This may take some of the wind out of the dreamer's sails, even as it conveys the message that you take the idea seriously enough to try to integrate it into the company's daily activities.

175. If it is impossible—or unwise—to say no to a bad idea, there is always the back burner. Respond to what seems an inherently unworkable notion with something like, "This is really interesting. Give me some time to think this through. I'll have a lot of questions for you." Such a response will not only buy you time—during which the idea may just die of natural causes—it will also give you the leisure actually to study the idea. You know, it is just possible that there *may* be something workable here.

176. Define an area of agreement before saying no: "You're certainly right that redesigning the logo would give us a fresh look, but I don't want to confuse consumers in the middle of the season. Let's wait at least four months before acting."

177. A colleague wants your support for her project. Trouble is, you think the idea is unworkable. How do you say no without alienating your colleague? If you really do care about the person, the *best* thing you can do for her is to explain your misgivings. Sure, it's difficult to tell somebody that their brainchild is ugly, but it is far crueler and potentially destructive to give false encouragement. "Alison, I've reviewed your idea, and I'd like to talk to you about it. I think, at the very least, that it needs more work."

178. Your boss is pushing a horrendous idea for a new product. You are certain that it is bound to fail. Trouble is, your boss wants to put you in charge of the program to develop the new product. The best way to say no to this idea is to do a great job as project leader—as long as you establish that your first objective will be to assess and report on the feasibility of the product. Avoid being tagged as a nay sayer—a danger you risk if you say no to the idea immediately—but, having defined the first part of your mission (to assess feasibility), set about marshaling the *facts* and research *data* you need to demonstrate that the new product idea is doomed.

179. If you think an idea is unworkable, say no to it—the idea—but not to the person who presents the idea. Never attack creativity. "That's a very creative solution, Liz, which is not surprising, since it comes from you. But it won't work because of the following three things . . ." After listing the difficulties, continue: "But I know that you'll come up with something that works."

180. Like junk, even a bad idea may have parts that you can salvage and recycle. Instead of saying no to it and turning your back, try to build on the idea. "This approach won't work because . . ." After listing the reasons, continue: "But if we take your idea and change it this way . . ." Then go on to build something feasible, giving generous credit to the builder of the original, albeit flawed, foundation.

NO
TO BLAME

181. It may not be mentioned in the first ten amendments to the United States Constitution, but you have the inalienable right to say no to blame for errors, snafues, and bad judgment calls that are not yours. But how do you avoid looking as if you're simply passing the buck or evading responsibility? The answer is to say no to blame without saying no to responsibility. Learn to accept situations that are not your fault but that are your responsibility. Begin by obtaining all of the information you need to respond appropriately to the situation, then approach the situation in the spirit of taking ownership of the problem—ownership, not blame.

182. Historians still debate whether World War II General Tomoyuki Yamashita should have been executed as a war criminal for the brutalities committed by his subordinates during Japan's last-ditch defense of Manila. Yamashita didn't order his men to commit atrocity, but a military tribunal ruled that a commander is ultimately responsible for the acts of his subordinates, whether or not they act on direct orders. Yamashita was hanged. Maybe you're no stranger to what the unfortunate general must have been feeling. Your subordinates may commit any number of "atrocities" for which you are not directly responsible, but which are nevertheless your problem. However, you *can* say no to accepting blame for these events without evading responsibility. If possible, resolve the situation without resorting to higher authority, but if you must make a report, demonstrate your willingness to shoulder the burden: "Mr. Hamilton, my shipping people didn't get the widget out by the deadline. We're going to be three days late. I want to send one of my installers out to you, at our expense, to expedite installation and gain back some of your lost time." If possible, avoid direct finger-pointing and naming names. You may apologize on behalf of those who work for you, but, far more than any apology, your supervisor or your customer wants responsible action that will alleviate any consequences of the snafu.

183. A variation on the supervisor or colleague who dishes out blame as if it were mashed potatoes at an all-you-can-eat diner is the person who, with similar generosity, ladles out the guilt. This individual is full of such passive-aggressive lines as "Don't trouble yourself," "No—really—we'll manage somehow without you," and "I can't expect you to do that." Whereas the bullying boss might imply that unless you do such-and-such, your job will be in jeopardy, the guilt-mongering boss insinuates that if such-and-such doesn't get done, you won't exactly lose your job, but the business will dissolve out from under *everyone*. Say no to guilt by learning to distinguish between emotion and necessity, between the guilt monger's feelings and what actually needs to be done. Is the deadline real, or is it in the guilt monger's mind? *Boss:* "Look, you go home. I'll just stay here and finish the report myself." *You:* "Do you really think that's necessary? You know, I'll be available all day tomorrow. I could rough out a draft then, and that would give you plenty of time to review it before the meeting on Wednesday."

184. You walk by Eunice Tompkins's desk. Eunice is never exactly friendly to you, but she's usually decent enough. Today, however, she stops you, twists her mouth into a particularly ugly expression, and accuses you of having lost a sale for her. She is steamed. It seems that you have a choice: vigorously defend yourself, or just stand there and take it. But there *is* a third alternative: *collect the facts.* When you are blindsided by blame, do not deny anything before gathering the full story. This will accomplish two things: first, it will calm the blamer down by shifting the focus from personalities to events; second, it will give you the time and space you need to demonstrate your blamelessness. Who knows, it may even lead to a resolution of the problem in question and thereby give you an opportunity to prove yourself not just guiltless, but a hero.

185. If you must deal daily with a habitual blamer, learn to focus on facts rather than personalities. Confront events rather than accusations. This will not be easy, because the last thing that interests the habitual blamer is fact. Her object is to shift responsibility from herself to you, and the facts may just get in the way.

186. In saying no to blame, be prepared nevertheless to accept responsibility. Make it clear that the snafu in question is not your *fault*, but that you are willing to take ownership of it as your *problem*. You will dig in and help resolve the situation. In this way, you have an opportunity to transform yourself from scapegoat to knight in shining armor.

187. Even when you do make a mistake, say no to blame. Do this by offering explanations instead of excuses. Sarah bent a company rule by showing a design to a client before securing final approval for it. Her boss, furious, confronted her. Fighting the impulse to make an excuse and deliver profuse apologies, Sarah instead provided an explanation: "Michael, the client was getting awfully anxious about the project, and I was afraid we'd lose him. I had to act quickly. Can I see you later this afternoon about this?"

188. Say no to blame by refusing to be left holding the bag. If you are required to stick your neck out, do whatever is prudent and appropriate to cover the part of your anatomy that lies at the opposite end of your torso. Act proactively. When you are required to make a risky decision, issue a memo explaining the decision, and be certain to get the necessary authorities and colleagues to *sign off* on the memo. This will avoid your being left to twist slowly, slowly in the wind in case a certain substance hits the fan.

"NO, BUT..." OFFERING ALTERNATIVES

189. To say no without rejecting either the request or the requester, provide alternatives.

190. In providing an alternative to an absolute no, be as specific as possible. Say: "I can't help you with this report, but I can work with you on the Smith report when that comes up in two weeks." Avoid being vague: "I can't. Maybe some other time."

191. Transform no into the firm foundation of great customer service by offering more than one helpful alternative. "I can't deliver the entire order by Tuesday, but I can offer you a choice of alternatives. I can deliver a partial order by Tuesday, with the balance to come Friday, or I can prepare the complete shipment here for you to pick it up on Tuesday."

192. *No* is an emotional black hole, the "0" component of a binary system. Whenever possible, transform the black-or-white world of *no* into a matter of degree: "We can't extend to you the $50,000 line of credit you request, but we can offer a $10,000 line at present. As we do more business together, we can revisit this limit."

193. It *is* possible to construct a firm *no* without sounding inflexible or unreasonable. Just be certain that you make clear the reasons for the *no* as well as the conditions under which a *yes* would be possible. "We can't extend credit to you at this time, because of your history of slow payment. If you are willing to let me, I'd like to take another look at your credit picture in six months, which should give you time to catch up on your open accounts. We'll reconsider the application then."

194. Perhaps the ultimate *no* is the no to a subordinate's continued employment with you: the termination. Before you take this step, consider the possibility of alternatives: "I have to tell you, Cynthia, that things are just not working out for you in sales. You work hard, and you are detail oriented—but it's clear that you are not comfortable selling. I do think that your knack with detail makes you a natural for customer service. Are you interested in discussing an alternative position?"

NO WHEN YOU'D LIKE TO SAY YES

195. Sometimes you want to issue an absolute, locked-down-tight no, and sometimes you want to leave the door open just a crack. In those cases, suggest future conditions under which a yes will be possible: "I'll be glad to help out when I don't have a schedule conflict."

196. If you've got good news, give 'em that first. Don't say, "Your credit application is incomplete. I can't process it." Instead, try: "I'm pleased to tell you that what you've submitted looks good. All I need to complete the application is three references from firms with which you regularly do business."

197. Many *nos* contain a *yes*. Try to find the *yes* and begin your response with it, rather than with the *no*. If Ms. Haygood requests X, and you are prepared to give Y, respond: "I can give you Y, but not X." Or you may not even have to mention the *no*: "I can give you Y, Ms. Haygood."

198. One of your subordinates asks you for an extra vacation day to spend time with a visiting family member. You'd like to say yes, but your company has an ironclad policy on vacation periods, and it is not within your power to authorize additional vacation time. Explain to the person that you understand her desire to spend time with her family, but that you don't have the authority to authorize additional vacation time. If possible, offer an alternative, perhaps telling her who in the management chain she could talk to. If you feel comfortable doing so, you might say something like, "Well, it is the cold and flu season. People do get sick, you know."

199. You'd like to make the deal, but you just don't have the funds to swing it. You have to say no. The one positive result that has come from this frustrating situation is that you've made contact with a supplier you'd like to do business with in the future. Let him know that: "Matt, I'm sorry we just couldn't swing this one. But, I promise you, there will be others. I am very impressed with what you bring to the table, and I look forward to doing business with you soon."

200. It is often helpful to shift the burden of the *no* to a third party. "If it were up to me. I could do that, but my manager just won't let me." However, beware of looking as if you are merely passing the buck.

201. Instead of simply issuing the *no*, analyze the *yes*. Explain to the other person how she could turn that no into a yes: "Look, Anne, I know you need help. If you can get sales of this line up by 5 percent before the end of the quarter, I can get you the executive assistant you want."